Hashtags for Business

Written by: Collin R. Maronese

I0464932

Disclaimer

While attempts have been made to verify information contained in this publication, neither the author nor the publisher assumes any responsibility for errors, omissions, interpretation, or usage of the subject matter herein. This publication contains the opinions and ideas of its author and is intended for informational purposes only and is meant to be a general guide. It is not intended, nor should be treated, as a definitive guide on the subject, nor should it be regarded as professional, legal, financial, or medical advice.

Please consult your own legal, financial, and/or medical advisor for professional advice relating to matters of your own specific situation.

The author and publisher shall in no event be held liable or be held responsible for any loss or other damages incurred from the usage of this publication, or for any problems/concerns that may arise, and will not be responsible for any loss, claim, or action from the information in this book.

Readers are encouraged to seek their own legal, financial, or medical advice before engaging in any activity on what they learn from this book.

Letter from the Author

"Focus on achieving one outcome towards greater success"

I realized that the world we live in today is rapidly changing, especially how we do business, and that excites me! You can never own success you can only rent it. I think it is important to know that as of right now in the social world, that the current trend may not be the trending "thing" it was yesterday. Hashtag's are a great example! This book can be used as a great tool for professional representation of your brand or business on social media platforms using hashtags. Business starts with two things, marketing and innovation. Buying this book and learning how social media has created this non-traditional movement in business, is being innovative!

To Your Success,

Collin R. Maronese

Contents

Introduction
Hashtags for Beginners

If you're a regular user of social media then I'm sure you've seen quite a few of those short phrased linked proceeded by a pound sign. Those are known by the social media world as hashtags. While they might seem confusing at first glance, hashtags play in integral role in the way people communicate on social media. Even if you're not a big fan, it's important that you learn how to use hashtags if you want to achieve the most success on social media.

Hashtags began with Twitter but have since spread to other platforms. When you post a hashtag, a link is created. This link will take users directly to a list of content that also uses the same hashtag. Think of it as an advanced way of creating categories for content on social media. For example, if you were watching an episode of Supernatural and wanted to post about it, then you would use the hashtag #Supernatural. This would group your post into the same category as others who are also posting about the same show.

You will be using these hashtags to make sure that your posts get included in the most effective categories. This book will walk you through the process of using hashtags for your business. By the end of this book, you will be able to use hashtags like a pro!

Platforms that Support Hashtags

What began with Twitter has spread like a wildfire to the rest of the social media world. Let's take a quick look at all of the supported platforms.

Twitter: Obviously, Twitter is the birthplace of the hashtag. Twitter still rules the world of hashtags and no other platform is even close. First of all, hashtags on Twitter are much more diverse than other websites. Twitter compiles a list of other hashtags that you might be interested in based on what you post.

You are also able search for hashtags on Twitter in three different ways:

> **Top** – Most popular topics relating to the hashtag. Includes users who you do not follow.

> **All** – Shows you every tweet that contains the hashtag in real time.

> **People you Follow** – Only shows you tweets that include the hashtag from people you follow.

Facebook: Facebook is relatively new to the world of hashtags. They added support back in June of 2013 but it has started to pick up a little steam. When you are on Facebook, you are shown a list of trending hashtags on the right of your news feed. If you click on a hashtag then you are taken to a list of posts that include that specific hashtag. There is no way to filter this list but your friends' posts are shown at the top of the list.

Instagram: Hashtags on Instagram are used to compliment any photos that you post. This helps users to discover new accounts to follow or to promote their pictures in an effort to pick up new followers. Some extremely popular trending hashtags were started on Instagram though – including the famous #TBT (Throwback Thursday) hashtag that is now used by millions of users every Thursday (or on random days by amateurs who post "#tbt to last weekend!" on a Monday).

Google+: By clicking on a hashtag within Google+, you will be shown a list of results that display several hashtags that include the specified hashtag. However, you are also shown posts that contain similar hashtags. Google also gives you the option of searching for trending hashtags within Twitter and Facebook.

Tumblr: Tumblr does hashtags differently from other social media platforms. You do not insert hashtags directly into posts. Instead, you are given a special section called "tags" where you can enter words or phrases. Each of these "tags" is then converted into a hashtag once you post the content.

Convey your Tone and Voice with Hashtags

Hashtags can be used for much more than simply organizing your posts. You can use them to craft your tone and voice when you join in large discussions by using more than one hashtag in a particular post. However, you do not want to go overboard. As a rule of thumb, never include more than three hashtags in a single post. By using multiple hashtags, you are able to provide more context to your post and convey different emotions like humor or sarcasm.

There are times when you will use a hashtag that is solely included to convey tone or sarcasm. Some hashtags might be so strange that there will not be many search results attached to it. I encourage you to use these types of hashtags sparingly. Sure, being whimsical is fun but if you do it too often, it becomes annoying to your followers.

Are Hashtags Here to Stay?

All of this brings up an interesting question. All of the evidence points to a definitive "yes." We can see just how integrated hashtags have become within all branches of social media. Since social media is clearly here to stay, then we can safely assume that hashtags are here for the long-term.

Hashtags play a pivotal role for all businesses. They create incentives for people to categorize posts, which makes it easier to find posts relating to a specific topic. It's also an easy way to distribute popular news to people who might not even be looking for it.

Chapter 1
Benefits of Hashtags for Business

Are you still feeling a bit intimidated or overwhelmed by hashtags? There is no better tool to beating intimidation than to face it head on. The truth is that hashtags have created a unique opportunity for businesses to network with consumers. They have unlocked a new way of marketing that cannot be ignored.

Twitter started this new trend and caused hashtags to become so popular that all other forms of social media had no choice but to incorporate them. There's a reason why they are so popular.

Hashtags Allow You to Join the Conversation!

Businesses use hashtags to increase their social presence by making sure that their voice is heard in all relevant conversations. Simply find a trending hashtag that relates to your target audience and then include that hashtag in a related post to improve brand awareness. Most of the social media platforms that you will be using will provide you with a list of trending hashtags. You can then seek out those that are relevant to your products and/or services, come up with an engaging post, and then let it rip!

Hashtags will allow you to improve the visibility of your business in a way that is unique, innovative, and memorable. Overall, posting to social media by using a popular hashtag allows users who might not even know that your company exists to access your content.

Hashtags Can be Used to Promote Special Events

Promotions and events are two key elements to any business. Most people love to save money through promotional offers or would be willing to join an event that your business is hosting. The problem is that many of those who are willing to join will never see your business. Hashtags create an interesting opportunity for promoting these types of special events.

Hashtags Allow you to Brand Your Business in a Unique Way

I'm sure that you already know the importance of branding. However, hashtags provide you with another unique branding opportunity. You can come up with your own original hashtag and then include it in all of your promotional posts. Just be sure that you keep it simple and leave users with enough room to include their thoughts. Hashtags create a unique method of branding that can really take off at an astonishing rate!

Hashtags Encourage Interaction

Hashtags provide a great way for fans to interact with your business. When you create hashtags that are original, then it must be something that is easy to remember, yet catchy. The easier a hashtag is to remember, the more likely it is to get included in posts. It must also be relevant to the product or service that it is promoting.

With that said, creating a hashtag that follows these guidelines allows you to engage your followers. It gives you an opportunity to address them and possibly even respond to their posts.

There are several ways that your business will benefit from hashtags so it's important that you make it a standard practice for all of your social media campaigns. If you are looking for innovative ways to reach new consumers, establish an online presence, and communicate with your customers then you need to start using hashtags.

Chapter 2

What Type of Business Benefits the Most from Hashtags?

So many businesses in today's digitally driven world are using hashtags to great success. Customers feel more comfortable with brands that they are able to connect with. That's why brands that effectively use social media tend to create the most trust from consumers. More trust means that you get more valuable customers for your business, as well as the ability to charge more for the product or service.

Some people seem to believe that the large companies dominate social media. However, the beauty of social media is that it presents a fair platform that allows small businesses to gain just as much exposure as large businesses. The real reason why you see most successful businesses effectively using hashtags is because they know just how powerful this feature is.

Have you ever wondered whether social media and hashtags will benefit your business? After all, who has the budget to compete with companies like Starbucks? That's might be the wrong question to ask since social media is not always about the dollars spent. It's more about the quality of time that you put into it.

Here's some good news for small business owners: hashtags are fair game for all businesses. Small businesses can benefit just as much as large corporations. So it's extremely important that your business is using hashtags as effectively as possible.

Social Media Continues to Evolve

Over the past five to six years, social media has transformed from an uncertain strategy to a primary marketing tool. Small businesses have benefitted the most from the emergence of social media. While large corporations have always had access to all other forms of media, small businesses have been limited in their marketing. As a result, it was difficult for them to achieve any substantial growth. Social media has provided an even playing field where no side really has a huge advantage over the other.

Social media continues to evolve as it grows. Its evolution has seen the emergence of photo sharing services like Instagram and video sharing services like YouTube. This evolutionary path eventually led to the emergence of hashtags, which also seem to benefit small businesses the most.

Hashtags help you to get your voice heard in a very noisy marketplace. Almost a whopping 90% of marketers see increased exposure from their social media campaigns by using hashtags. The remaining 10% only fail to see this increase because they are not using them correctly.

Your Investment is in Time

One of the greatest benefits of using hashtags for your

business is that most of your investment will be in time, not money. That can also be a double-edged sword for small business owners though. If you're like me, then you have a lot of demand for your time. Marketing is just one of the many hats that you're forced to wear. This is where I give you even more great news.

Your investment in time will pay huge dividends.

The key is consistency and endurance. Consistency is required to keep your followers engaged while endurance is required to build your list of followers. You only need to spend about 6 hours per week on social media and most of that time will be to develop posts and engage with followers. Hashtags will take a small chunk of that time – probably about 15 minutes per day.

Committing six hours of your week to social media is a great goal to set. Be sure that of those six hours, you are devoting at least 15 minutes per day to finding the best hashtags to use.

The Four Tools that Lead to Success

All marketers have a toolkit that they use for their online marketing campaigns. One of the problems that many small business owners make is that they overwhelm themselves by using too many tools. I encourage you to focus your efforts on these four:

Collin R. Maronese

➢ Twitter

➢ Facebook

➢ LinkedIn

➢ Blogs

Your goal is to funnel all of your Twitter, Facebook, and LinkedIn leads to your blog. Your blog is what converts leads into customers.

The Bottom Line

Keeping everything you have just read in mind, you can clearly see that small businesses benefit the most from hashtags since it gives them a rare opportunity to compete with large corporations.

Chapter 3
How to Correctly Use Hashtags

Every successful business in the world has an established social media presence. Most of these businesses use hashtags to promote specific events so you need to be doing the same. The best part is that you do not have to start from scratch here. There is no need to reinvent the wheel. The road has already been paved by successful entrepreneurs so you can just follow the guidelines that have already been established. This chapter will show you several tips that will help you learn to effective use hashtags to grow your list of consumers.

Only Certain Characters are Allowed in Hashtags
Let's start with the basics.

One of the most common mistakes that I see on social media is where beginners include a space in a hashtag. Spaces are not allowed, even if the hashtag includes multiple words.

Correct - #BestDeals or #bestdeals

Incorrect - #Best Deals

I recommend that you use capital letters to differentiate the words in a phrased hashtag. While it's not required, you can see in the example above that using capital letters to differentiate words in a hashtag makes it look more professional. Finally, since hashtags are not case sensitive, #BestDeals and #bestdeals would be grouped under the same hashtag.

Numbers are allowed with hashtags so don't be afraid to include #Top10Lists in your posts.

Punctuation marks are not supported. Leave out any punctuation marks, including apostrophes.

I also feel it's worth mentioning that the @ symbol is completely different from the #. They both do completely different things. The hashtag (#) symbol will link your post to a specific category while using the @ symbol before a person's name will direct the post at that person. Sometimes users will hashtag and post directly to a celebrity. Using the @ makes the post appear on the user's feed.

Using Hashtags for Business

Now that we've got the basics out of the way, let's focus on some of the more advanced tips on correctly using hashtags.

1. Use Hashtags that are Relevant to Your Business

Do your homework and research companies that are in the same niche as yours. Pay attention to what hashtags they are using and model them. Write down your favorite ones for use with your future posts.

2. Always Pay Attention to What's Trending

Sure, you want your business to be completely unique but that doesn't mean that you can ignore trends in favor of uniqueness. On the contrary, trends create a great opportunity to engage with a lot of consumers. When you see a trend that is related to your business, be sure to post something that uses that trending hashtag. Do it quickly since trends change at a rapid pace.

3. Consolidate your Posts

Set up social media accounts that are specifically designed for your business. You cannot use a personal social media account to effectively promote your business. Yet, I see so many people try and do just that. Before you even start using hashtags, you need to make sure that you have a separate account for your business on each platform. Then consolidate your posts using that single account.

4. Practice Creating your Own Hashtags

Eventually, you are going to create your own hashtags to use with your social media campaigns so you might as well start practicing. We will discuss this in more detail later but for now just practice thinking up unique, catchy hashtags for use with your business. Write them down.

5. Hashtags Should Generate Buzz

Create contests or other promotions around a hashtag. This helps you to generate buzz around your posts and gets people talking about it. For example, a user might be more motivated to share your post if you give them a reward for doing so.

6. Make Sure your Privacy Settings are Public

This is actually a common mistake. Sometimes, we are so worried about privacy that we set up our social media accounts in a way that keeps hashtags from being seen by all users like they should. Make sure your account is set to *Public* so that everyone can see your posts.

7. Your Hashtag Post Should be Specific

When you use a hashtag to join in on a conversation, then make sure that the post is specific and related to the topic. Try to avoid unrelated or vague hashtags.

8. Never Use too Many Hashtags

If you include too many hashtags in a post, it comes across as spam. As I mentioned earlier, never include more than three hashtags in a single post. Also, never include the same hashtag more than once in the same post.

Note: You can use more than three tags on Instagram, Vine, and YouTube.

9. Provide Context

Have you ever come across a post that included only hashtags? I'm sure you have and it probably drew the same response from you as it did for me: it was a head scratcher! Don't do this. Not only is it confusing, but it doesn't add anything to the conversation. Your followers will have no idea what you are talking about.

10. Learn to Advertise on Trending Hashtags

This is where you will be focusing most of your efforts as you start using hashtags. Learn how to create posts that are based on trending hashtags so that you get the most exposure. However, you must always remember one key word here – relevance. Never try to force yourself onto a trending topic that has no relevance to your business. Irrelevant posts on a trending topic are seen as spam. If you do it right then you can ride huge trends all the way to the bank.

11. Hashtag Tracking and Analytics

When you are searching for hashtags to use, the ability to track and analyze trending topics is a huge advantage. Hashtags.org is a good tool for accomplishing this goal. Find popular trending hashtags that are associated with your brand and then include them in your posts.

You can also use these types of tools to see how well your posts are converting by tracking their social reach.

12. Use Hashtags Consistently Across All Platforms

Not only should you use hashtags across all social media platforms, you need to be consistent. For example, when you are using a trending hashtag then you should be posting it on Twitter, Facebook, Google+, and all other social media platforms that are included in your marketing campaign.

Chapter 4
How to Identify Hashtags for Your Business

Using the right hashtags is critical to your social media campaign so it serves as a logical starting point for our step-by-step process. Using the right hashtags will allow you to join in on conversations that are already engaging your target audience. We are going to be using three popular programs to identify hashtags that are perfect for your business.

Step 1: Build a Starter List of Hashtags

We are starting out from a completely fresh perspective. In order to use this step, you will need to be actively using Twitter. I will assume that you are using Twitter. If you're not, then you should be.

1. Visit http://www.twitonomy.com/

2. Log into your Twitter Account to authorize the app.

3. Your Twitter Account is then analyzed and you are given a list of hashtags. Write down all of these hashtags. This will be your **Starter List of Hashtags**.

Step 2: Identify Hashtags Related to Your Starter List

Next, we are going to head over to another website. I like to use multiple sources for research so that I can ensure that it is accurate and diverse.

1. Visit http://hashtagify.me/

2. Type in a hashtag from your **Starter List of Hashtags** into the **Search Bar** shown below. For our example, we are going to use the hashtag **#SocialMedia.**

3. You will be given a list of related hashtags. Write down any of these hashtags that are related to your business.

4. Repeat Steps 2 + 3 for every hashtag on your **Starter List of Hashtags**.

Step 3: Review your New List for Relevance

Now I want you to go back through your list of hashtags and gauge their relevance once again. Choose no more than 20 hashtags that are the best fit for your business.

- **Avoid Hashtags that are Too General.** Using the example above, hashtags like **#Facebook** and **#Twitter** are too general to be effective.

- **Avoid Unrelated Hashtags:** If you are promoting a news blog, then **#marketing** might be irrelevant.

Step 4: Test Your Hashtags

Once you have a working list, you will then need to see what types of companies are sending out posts related to your hashtags.

1. Sign up for a free HootSuite Account at the following link: https://hootsuite.com/plans/free

2. Set up a stream for your hashtags so that you can see all posts that contain each hashtag. You have two goals here:

- To ensure that companies that are related to yours are using the hashtag.

- Consumers who match your target audience are using the hashtag.

How to Find Trending Hashtags

Why not take advantage of hashtags that are already trending? This is an opportunity that you cannot afford to miss so we will end this chapter with a quick look at finding good, trending hashtags. I recommend that you follow through with this every day and take advantage of trends.

1. Visit https://www.hashtags.org/. I recommend that you sign up for a free account so that you can get the most from this powerful website.

2. You are shown a massive list of trending hashtags. You are looking for hashtags that relate to your business. Don't be afraid to get creative.

For example, holiday hashtags are a great way to join in conversations and offer promotions. While your company

Hashtags for Beginners

might not be related to **#Easter**, you can still offer discounts or have contests on this popular holiday and post about them using the hashtag **#Easter**.

Chapter 5
Hashtag Business Strategies

Creating a list of hashtags is the first step to growing your social media campaign but now we need to get more specific. After all, what good is it to have a list if you don't use it? This chapter is going to show you a few hashtag strategies that you can start using immediately. Are you ready to get started?

Establish a Brand Hashtag

A **Brand Hashtag** is a unique hashtag that you create for your business. Then you will use it to market your own products. Many people use their company name but I do not recommend this. Instead, use your company tagline as your brand hashtag. Create a hashtag that defines your entire business in just a few short words.

The advantage of creating a brand hashtag is that you can use it to create buzz around your products and services. If you can get others to use this hashtag, then they are marketing for you. I will admit that creating a tagline is one of the most difficult steps to effectively marketing your business but it is absolutely necessary. If you don't have a tagline then you should create one.

This tagline will become your brand hashtag. You will include it in every post that relates to your business. Eventually, your customers will start using it. A brand hashtag can take off at a moment's notice! Here are a few guidelines that you should follow.

Always make sure that your brand hashtag is unique. Search for it to ensure that no other company is using the same hashtag. If you find that someone is already using it, then you will have to create another one.

Keep your brand hashtag short so that it's easy to remember. You want your followers to remember your brand hashtag. You also want them to be able to easily spell it correctly. For example, if you are a logo design company then you would not want to use a brand hashtag like **#bestlogodesignsinthebusiness**. Instead, use something short like **#discountlogos**.

> ➢ Keep your brand hashtag simple and unique.

> ➢ Use your brand hashtag on all of your social media sites, as well as all other forms of marketing.

> ➢ Monitor your brand hashtag and try to respond to your followers from time-to-time.

Using a Campaign Hashtag

A campaign hashtag is a short-term tagline used to describe a specific promotion. Make it a word or phrase that is catchy and unique. Again, do your homework. If the hashtag that you have chosen is already being used by another company then choose a different campaign tag.

You use campaign hashtags as a way for your customers to interact with each other and with your brand throughout the duration of the entire offer. It's a very important tactic to learn. What most companies do is require customers to post something using the hashtag in order to enter a contest or ask them to post using the hashtag after they have made a purchase.

One popular example of a hashtag campaign is a photo contest. If you are a regular user of Facebook, Twitter, or Instagram then you have probably seen one of your favorite brands host one of these photo contests. This contest requires you to take a photo and tag it with a specific hashtag. Then they will present a number of selected winners. That is a hashtag campaign. The company gives customers a fun and unique way of winning prizes. In return, the company gets thousands of unique images of people using their product and the wide-spread use of their campaign hashtag.

- ➢ When you decide to use a campaign hashtag, you should use it on as many social media sites as possible.

- ➢ Like with a brand hashtag, your campaign tag needs to be something that is simple and easy to remember.

- ➢ Create a campaign hashtag to use with every promotion or contest so that you can generate more buzz around it.

Strategy for Using Trending Hashtags

Trending hashtags are those that have already become very popular. You might have heard others talking about trends or saw the *"Trending"* section on Facebook. These are hashtags that are trending across the world. In essence, they are the topics that the most people are discussing.

Trending hashtags come and go within minutes. No joke; a topic that is in the top 10 can fall out of the top 100 in just a few minutes. It's that fast! That makes it important to try your best to keep up with what's trending.

When you find a hashtag that is trending, then you need to engage it as soon as possible. You will have the potential of having your post seen by a massive amount of people. The best part about using trending hashtags is that your posts are seen by people who are outside of your current list of followers. Plus, it's a completely free method of reaching these people. Think of it as your company's way to get *15 seconds of fame.*

Never spam trending hashtags though or else you could suffer severe consequences. Posting too many trends is seen as poor business etiquette. This is also true when you start posting in trends that do not relate to your business. Spamming can lead to a loss of followers or worse – your social media account can get suspended.

Finding a Trending Hashtag

Most social media sites have an easy way to view trending

topics. On Facebook, it's to the right of your news feed. On Twitter, it's to the left of your Twitter feed. Sometimes you can even change the trends so that they are filtered by geographic location, which is a huge benefit.

With that said, I do not recommend that you use those methods to find trending hashtags. Instead, use one of the following resources to get a more in-depth analysis.

Hashtags.org

This is a great tool that I mentioned earlier in this book. Use it to find trending hashtags. You can use it to filter trending topics by niche as well. Hashtags.org can also be used to determine which trending topics have begun to decline and which ones are growing. Naturally, you want to find trends that are growing.

Trendsmap.com

Trendsmap is a truly awesome tool that is set up like a map. It will then show you trending topics in different areas of the world. If you are looking to grow your local presence, then Trendsmap is a great way to find hashtags that are trending in your area.

Using a Trending Hashtag

Start off by closely monitoring trends using the methods we just went through. When you see a trend that relates to your business, create a unique post that includes the hashtag. You can be creative here. For example, Oreo sent out a tweet when **#FashionWeek** was a trending topic.

"Why all black? Because all white was sooooooo last week."
#FashionWeek

As you can see, that post was creative on so many levels. It promoted the Oreo brand, plus it was catchy and memorable. Sure, Oreo has nothing to do with fashion but they were still able to have fun with it.

With that said, there is another type of trend called niche trending. By using a popular niche hashtag, you are able to get your posts seen by like-minded people. The goal with niche trends is to get your posts seen by consumers who are using the same hashtag.

Some popular examples of niche trending hashtags includes:

#MusicMonday – This trend began on Google+ but has spread to other social media outlets over time. It's used to promote music related posts on Mondays.

#ThrowBackThursday – This trend encourages users to post pictures of things related to the past. Most people use older pictures of themselves but some companies get creative and show past events. Whatever the case, Throwback Thursday has become quite popular.

#TGIF – Everyone knows what TGIF means. It's a niche trend where people show their love for Friday.

There are thousands of niche trends including holidays, social events, and much more. The more you actively use social media, the better you will become at finding these niche trending hashtags.

➢ You must be quick when using a trending hashtag. The quicker you post a trending hashtag, the more exposure your post will get. Remember, trending hashtags decline very quickly.

➢ Find trending topics using hashtags.org or TrendsMap. Avoid relying on the trending topics as shown on social media sites. By the time it makes this list, it has already reached its peak.

➢ Take part in niche trending hashtags so that you can connect with your target market and develop a relationship with them.

Content Hashtags

Finally, we come to content hashtags that are used solely to categorize your posts. They are not branded, nor are they used to define your business. They are not trending topics. They are simply tags used to group your posts to other related posts.

Content hashtags have an important job though – they improve the SEO (search engine optimization) of your posts. They make your posts visible to users who are performing searches for the particular tag you use. Some content hashtags might include **#socialmedia** or **#marketingtips**.

Content hashtags are the SEO keywords of the social media world.

There are thousands of content hashtags that you could use, but most of them fall under one of the following categories:

- ➢ Lifestyle hashtags
- ➢ Event hashtags
- ➢ Product hashtags
- ➢ Location hashtags

Let's look at these four categories in more detail.

Lifestyle Hashtags
People love connecting with others who share a similar lifestyle. That's where demographics and hashtags connect. To market using lifestyle hashtags, you need to know what type of lifestyle your target audience leads. Then seek some commonly used hashtags that meet this lifestyle and include them in your updates.

Event Hashtags
Event hashtags are an extraordinary tactic if used correctly. You can use local events or well-known global celebrations. Heck, you can even create event hashtags to promote your own product launches of webinars. However, since this book

is designed for beginners, I recommend that you stick with other events until you become more experienced with using hashtags.

Product Hashtags

Everyone uses products so you can bet that these same people are going to search product hashtags to find them. When you are posting a product or service for your business, then put yourself into the shoes of the customer. What would they search for if they needed your product or service? Use product hashtags to connect the dots.

Location Hashtags

This hashtag is best reserved for businesses that need to connect with local customers. Use location hashtags only if you are looking to get new local customers. If you post something with a location hashtag, then people within that location are going to see it.

➢ Search for common hashtags that are being used by your target market, your competition, and your partners.

➢ Engage with your followers by including these common hashtags in your posts. You can even include them when you comment on another post.

➢ Never spam posts with too many hashtags. This is easy to do when you start using common hashtags. Use only one or two common hashtags per post if you want the best effect.

Hashtags for Beginners

Final Thoughts

No matter what type of business you own, your social media campaigns will benefit from the use of hashtags. The key is to use these hashtags correctly. When done right, hashtags are one of the best ways to create new lines of communication with your target market.

By now, you should have a definitive method to start using hashtags for your business. So I encourage you to start developing new social media marketing strategies that gradually work these hashtags into your normal posts. Always start out small and then gradually build on it. Before you know it, you'll be using every type of business hashtag mentioned in this book.

The best way to finish this book is to provide a brief checklist of everything you should have learned in this book.

➢ If you are not using hashtags with your social media campaign, then start now. Hashtags provide a level playing field for small businesses to compete against large corporations. They are too beneficial to be ignored!

➢ Hashtags get you in on the conversation, allow you a free way to promote your business, and can even brand your business in a unique way.

➢ It's important that you use hashtags correctly. By not following the specifications mentioned in this book, you run the risk of coming across as unprofessional. In fact, the incorrect use of hashtags can actually lead to a loss of followers.

➢ Identify hashtags for your business first by using tools like hashtags.org and trendsmap.com. Trend lists that are created on social media sites show you hashtags that have already reached the peak of their trend. Your goal is to find hashtags that are still trending.

➢ Never, under any circumstances, include more than three hashtags in a single post.

➢ Create a **Brand Hashtag** that is unique to your business.

➢ Develop written strategies for using hashtags. You will need to set up three strategies: brand, trending, and common hashtags should all be treated differently.

Above all else, make sure that you start right now! Do not put it off another day. A common mistake that so many small business owners fall prey to is that they do not put what they learn into practice. Hashtags are no longer optional – they are a necessity for small businesses looking to harness the power of social media marketing.

About the Author

Collin R. Maronese is an entrepreneurship visionary. At the age of 12, he made around $2,000 by selling anything from magic cards, pixie sticks, GameCube games, and tech deck dudes (if you remember those toys) on the playground, to paintball guns, pedal bike accessories and riding gear online. Not only did he love making money, he loved people and strived to build long-lasting valuable bonds with everyone he met and currently meets.

This book is his first step taken towards writing valuable content in the 21st century for business. Currently, he is 21 and has completed three out of four years in the HB Commerce program in Thunder Bay ON, Canada majoring in marketing and minoring in finance. He likes to compare himself to a well-known business term Customer Relationship Management (CRM) as they are his initials, but also the very key development concept that holds his work with others together.